Great Women

and their words of wisdom

Compiled by Michael Ritter

Published by
Great Quotations Publishing Co.,
Glendale Heights, IL

ISBN 1-56245-212-6

Printed in Hong Kong

Table of Contents

Introduction

Women have always had a lot to say, but they haven't always had a chance to be heard. Many of the women quoted in this book had no way of knowing that their words would outlive them and inspire so many. We hope that you are as encouraged and enlightened as we have in putting together this wonderful collection of quotes from some of the most prominent and influencial women in history.

<u>Chapter 1</u>

Reach For The Stars

What are we doing here?
We're reaching for the stars.
- Christa McAuliffe
(1948 - 1986)

The first teacher in space, Christa McAuliffe had intended to conduct lessons from the Challenger. The nation witnessed a great tragedy when the shuttle burst into flames.

Far away there in the sunshine are my highest aspirations. I may not reach them, but I can look up and see their beauty, believe in them and try to follow where they lead.

- Louisa May Alcott
(1832 - 1888)
American writer

Nothing in life is to be feared.
It is only to be understood.
                    - Marie Curie
                    (1867 - 1934)

Twice winning the Nobel
Prize, Marie Curie's
contributions to nuclear
physics have paved the way
for the development of the
treatment of illness through
intense radioactive sources.

I do not know anyone who has got to the top without hard work. That is the recipe. It will not always get you to the top, but it should get you pretty near.

- Margaret Thatcher
(1925 -)

Known as the "Iron Lady", Margaret Thatcher became the first woman in European history to be elected prime minister.

I am only one; but still I am one. I cannot do everything, but still I can do something; I will not refuse to do the something I can do.

- Helen Keller
(1880 - 1968)

Illness in her infancy left Helen Keller without sight, hearing or the ability to speak. Through the patient instruction of Anne Sullivan, Helen Keller learned to write and speak. She went on to graduate Cum Laude from Radcliffe College in 1904.

Challenges make you discover
things about yourself that you
never really knew. They're
what make the instrument
stretch - what makes you go
beyond the norm.

- Cicely Tyson
(1939 -)
American actress

All serious daring starts from within.

          - Eudora Welty
            (1909 -)
        American writer

I learned...that inspiration does not come like a bolt, nor is it kinetic, energetic striving, but it comes into us slowly and quietly and all the time, though we must regularly and every day give it a little chance to start flowing, prime it with a little solitude and idleness.

          - Brenda Ueland
          (1891 - 1985)
        American writer

If you really want to reach for the brass ring, just remember that there are sacrifices that go along.

- Cathleen Black
(1944 -)
American publisher

To attempt to climb - to achieve - without a firm objective in life is to attain nothing.

- Mary G. Roebling
(1905)
American businesswoman

The strongest desire known to human life is to continue living. The next strongest is to use the instruments by which life is generated for its own rewards, not for the sake of generation. The third potent desire is to excel and be acknowledged.

- Dorothy Dudley
(1905 -)
American writer

There are only two ways of spreading light - to be the candle or the mirror that reflects it.

- Edith Wharton
(1862 - 1937)
American novelist, critic

The very commonplaces of life
are components of its eternal
mystery.
- Gertrue Franklin Atherton
(1857 - 1948)
American novelist

Only she who attempts the
absurd can achieve the
impossible.
- Sharon Lee Schuster
(1939 -)
American executive

There is nothing in the universe that I fear, but that I shall not know all my duty, or shall fail to do it.

- Mary Lyon
(1797 - 1849)
American educator

Imagination is the highest kite one can fly.

- Lauren Bacall
(1924 -)
American actress

Don't be afraid of the space
between your dreams and
reality. If you can dream it,
you can make it so.
                        - Belva Davis
                        (contemporary)
                    American newscaster

We must overcome the notion
that we must be regular...it
robs you of the chance to be
extraordinary and leads you
to be mediocre.
                        - Uta Hagen
                        (1919 -)
                    German/American actress,
                        educator

CHAPTER 2

Diamonds in the Rough

Success can make you go one of two ways. It can make you a prima donna, or it can smooth out the edges, take away the insecurities, let the nice things come out.
- Barbara Walters (1931 -)
U.S. journalist, writer,
television producer and
commentator

Diamonds are only chunks of coal that stuck to their jobs, you see.

> \- Minnie Richard Smith
> (19th c.)
> American poet

If enough people think of a thing and work hard enough at it, I guess it's pretty nearly bound to happen, wind and weather permitting.

> \- Laura Ingalls Wilder
> (1867 - 1957)
> American writer

If you think you can, you can.
And if you think you can't,
you're right.
- Mary Kay Ash (1915 -)
American businesswoman

Life is to be lived. If you have
to support yourself, you had
bloody well better find some
way that is going to be
interesting. And you don't do
that by sitting around
wondering about yourself.
- Katharine Hepburn
(1907 -)
American actress

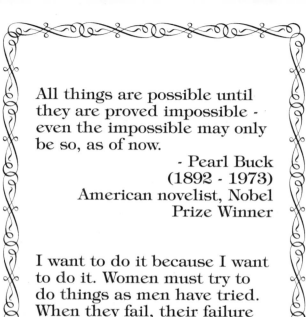

All things are possible until
they are proved impossible -
even the impossible may only
be so, as of now.

- Pearl Buck
(1892 - 1973)
American novelist, Nobel
Prize Winner

I want to do it because I want
to do it. Women must try to
do things as men have tried.
When they fail, their failure
must be a challenge to others.
- Amelia Earhart
(1898 - 1937)
American aviation pioneer

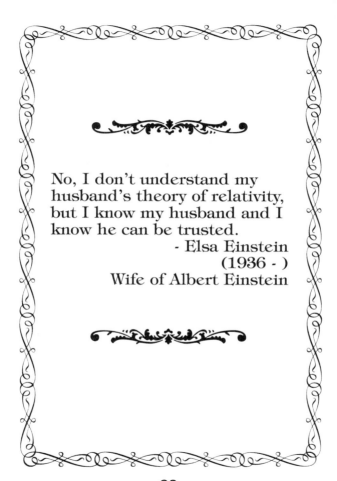

No, I don't understand my husband's theory of relativity, but I know my husband and I know he can be trusted.
- Elsa Einstein
(1936 -)
Wife of Albert Einstein

If I'm such a legend, why am I so lonely?

> — Judy Garland
> (1922 - 1969)
> American singer and actress

Reality is something you rise above.

> — Liza Minnelli
> (1946 -)
> U.S. actress and singer.Daughter of Judy Garland

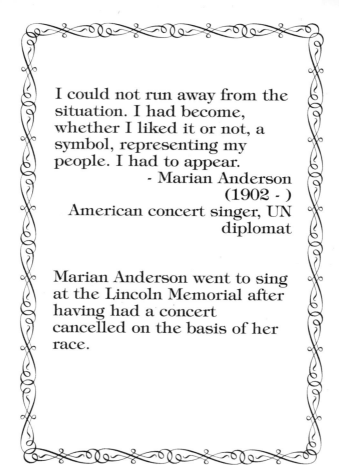

I could not run away from the situation. I had become, whether I liked it or not, a symbol, representing my people. I had to appear.
- Marian Anderson
(1902 -)
American concert singer, UN diplomat

Marian Anderson went to sing at the Lincoln Memorial after having had a concert cancelled on the basis of her race.

I wanted a perfect
ending....Now I've learned,
the hard way, that some
poems don't rhyme, and some
stories don't have a clear
beginning, middle and end.
Life is about not knowing,
having to change, taking the
moment and making the best
of it, without knowing what's
going to happen next.
Delicious ambiguity.

- Gilda Radner
  (1946 - 1989)
  American comedienne

Life is what we make it,
always has been, always will
be.

- Grandma Moses
(Anna Mary Robertson Moses,
1860 - 1961)
American painter

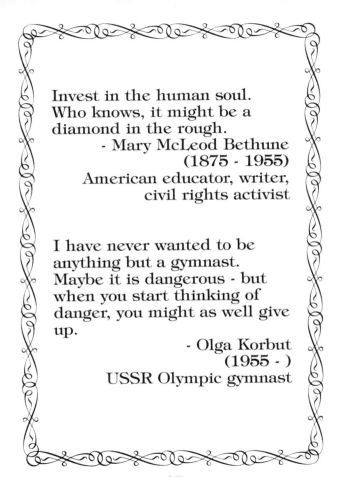

Invest in the human soul.
Who knows, it might be a
diamond in the rough.
- Mary McLeod Bethune
(1875 - 1955)
American educator, writer,
civil rights activist

I have never wanted to be
anything but a gymnast.
Maybe it is dangerous - but
when you start thinking of
danger, you might as well give
up.
- Olga Korbut
(1955 -)
USSR Olympic gymnast

I listen and give input only if
somebody asks.
- Barbara Bush
(1925 -)
Former First Lady of the
United States and
humanitarian

Men their rights and nothing
more; women their rights and
nothing less.
- Susan Brownell
Anthony
(1820 - 1906)

Best remembered for paving
the way for the Nineteenth
Amendment to the United
States Constitution, which
gave women the right to vote.

I had reasoned this out in my mind, there were two things I had a right to: liberty and death. If I could not have one, I would have the other, for no man should have take me alive.

- Harriet Tubman
(1820 - 1913)

Born into slavery, Harriet Tubman yearned to be free. In 1849, she escaped to Pennsylvania through the Underground Railroad. She then used the same route to return to the South and help more than 300 slaves to freedom.

I'm having trouble managing the mansion. What I need is a wife.

- Ella Tambussi Grasso
(1919 -)
The first woman to become a U.S. Governor (Connecticut)

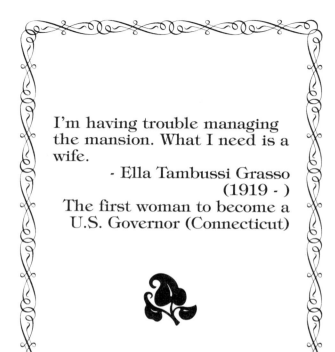

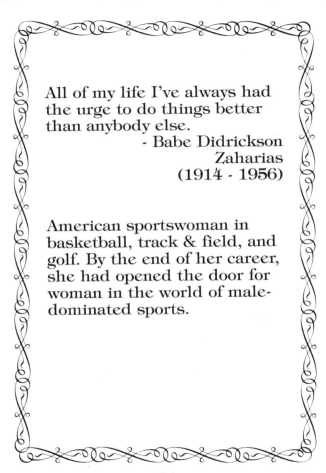

All of my life I've always had the urge to do things better than anybody else.

> - Babe Didrickson
> Zaharias
> (1914 - 1956)

American sportswoman in basketball, track & field, and golf. By the end of her career, she had opened the door for woman in the world of male-dominated sports.

CHAPTER 3

Opportunity Knocks

Luck is a matter of
preparation meeting
opportunity.
- Oprah Winfrey (1953 -)
American talk show host,
producer, actress

Opportunities are usually
disguised by hard work, so
most people don't recognize
them.
- Ann Landers (Esther
Friedman, 1918 -)
American advice columnist

I wasn't afraid to fail.
Something good always comes
out of failure.

> \- Anne Baxter
> (1923 -)
> American actress

The time you need to do
something is when no one
else is willing to do it, when
people are saying it can't be
done.

> \- Mary Frances Berry
> (1938 -)
> American history and law
> professor

Action is the antidote to
despair.

> \- Joan Baez
> (1941 -)
> American folk singer, civil
> rights activist, pacifist

It had long since come to my
attention that people of
accomplishment rarely sat
back and let things happen to
them. They went out and
happened to things.

> \- Elinor Smith
> (1917 -)
> American writer

You may be disappointed if you fail, but you are doomed if you don't try.

- Beverly Sills
(Belle Miriam Silverman Greenough, "Bubbles", 1929-)
American opera singer, administrator

Don't wait for your "ship to come in", and feel angry and cheated when it doesn't. Get going with something small.

- Dr. Irene Kassorla
(1931 -)
American psychologist, writer

Just go out there and do what
you've got to do.
- Martina Navratilova
(1956 -)
Czechoslavakian/American
tennis champion

You've got to take the
initiative and play your
game...confidence makes the
difference.
- Chris Evert
(1954 -)
American tennis champion

Security is not the meaning of my life. Great opportunities are worth the risks.

> \- Shirley Hufstedler
> (1926 -)
> American lawyer, judge,
> Secretary of Education

Unfortunately, history is not on our side. No society in history has ever made the successful transition from leader of one economic era to leader of a new economic era. They've usually failed because they've jumped too late.

> \- Christine D. Keen
> (contemporary)
> American businesswoman

The English word "crisis" is translated by the Chinese with two little characters; one means "danger" and the other "opportunity".
- Jean Hougk
(1947 -)
American clinical social worker

There are no problems - only opportunities to be creative.
- Dorye Roettger
(1932 -)
American author, public speaker

I don't know anything about luck. I've never banked on it, and I'm afraid of people who do. Luck to me is something else: hard work and realizing what is opportunity and what isn't.

-Lucille Ball
(1911 - 1989)
American comedienne, TV
personality

One can present people with opportunities. One cannot make them equal to them.
- Rosamund Lehman
(1901 - 1990)
English novelist

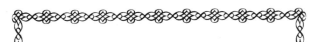

When so rich a harvest is before us, why do we not gather it? All is in our hands if we will but use it.

- Elizabeth Seton
(1774-1821)
First American Saint

When you get into a tight place and it seems you can't go on, hold on, for that's just the place and the time that the tide will turn.

- Harriet Elizabeth
Beecher Stowe
(1811 - 1896)
U.S. novelist, abolitionist, social reformer, theologian

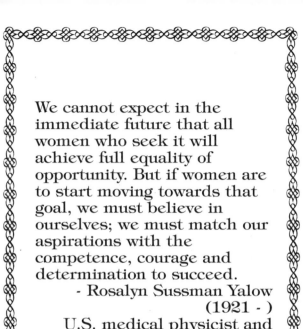

We cannot expect in the immediate future that all women who seek it will achieve full equality of opportunity. But if women are to start moving towards that goal, we must believe in ourselves; we must match our aspirations with the competence, courage and determination to succeed.
- Rosalyn Sussman Yalow
(1921 -)
U.S. medical physicist and shared winner of 1977 Nobel Prize for Medicine

There is a spirit and a need
and a man at the beginning of
every great human advance.
Every one of these must be
right for that particular
moment of history, or nothing
happens.

- Coretta Scott King
(1927 -)
American writer and civil
rights activist

CHAPTER 4

Secrets of Success

I've always believed that one
woman's success can only
help another women's
success.
- Gloria Vanderbilt
(1924 -)
American artist, writer,
designer

Success is counted sweetest
By those who ne'er succeed.
- Emily Dickinson
(1830 - 1886)
American poet

What really matters is what
you do with what you have.
- Shirley Lord
(contemporary)
American writer, magazine
editor

You are the product of your
own brainstorm.
- Rosemary Konner
Steinbaum
(1952 -)
American educator

I am suffocated and lost when
I have not the bright feeling
of progression.

> \- Margaret Fuller
> (1810 - 1850)
> American writer, journalist,
> editor, poet, critic

I've never sought success in
order to get fame and money;
it's the talent and the passion
that count in success.

> \- Ingrid Bergman
> (1915 - 1982)
> Swedish actress and
> playwright

I stopped believing in Santa
Claus when I was six. Mother
took me to see him in a
department store and he
asked for my autograph.
- Shirley Temple Black
(1928 -)
American actress, diplomat

The worst part of success is to
try to finding someone who is
happy for you.
- Bette Midler
(1945 -)
American singer, actress,
comedienne

Figure out what your most magnificent qualities are and make them indispensable to the people you want to work with. Notice I didn't say "work for".
- Linda Bloodworth-Thomason
                    (contemporary)
        American TV producer

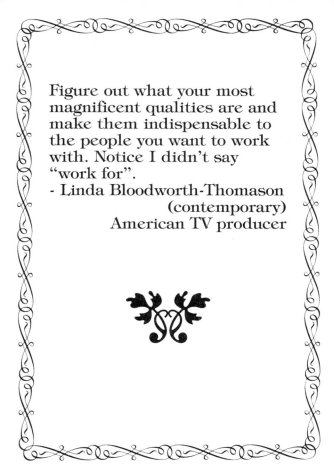

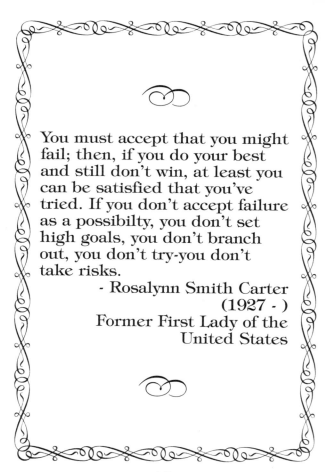

You must accept that you might fail; then, if you do your best and still don't win, at least you can be satisfied that you've tried. If you don't accept failure as a possibilty, you don't set high goals, you don't branch out, you don't try-you don't take risks.

- Rosalynn Smith Carter
(1927 -)
Former First Lady of the
United States

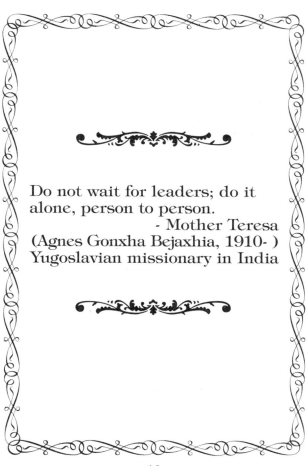

Do not wait for leaders; do it alone, person to person.
              - Mother Teresa
(Agnes Gonxha Bejaxhia, 1910-)
Yugoslavian missionary in India

Getting ahead in a difficult profession requires avid faith in yourself. That is why some people with mediocre talent, but with great inner drive, go much further than people with vastly superior talent.

- Sophia Loren
(1934 -)
Italian actress

The excellent becomes the permanent.

Jane Addams
(1860 - 1935)
American humanitarian, reformer, settlement house founder, sociologist, Nobel Prize winner

I hope I have convinced you -
the only thing that separates
successful people from the
ones who aren't is the
willingness to work very, very
hard.

- Helen Gurley Brown
(1922 -)
American publisher, author

Life is a succession of
moments. To live each one is
to succeed.

- Corita Kent
(1918)
American graphic artist

To be successful, the first thing to do is is fall in love with your work.
- Sister Mary Lauretta
(contemporary)

The only place you find success before work is in the dictionary.
- May V. Smith
(1922 -)
American government worker

If you have made mistakes, even serious ones, there is always another chance for you. What we call failure is not the falling down, but the staying down.
- Mary Pickford
(1893 - 1979)
Canadian-born U.S. actress

CHAPTER 5

Love and Relationships

The story of a love is not important - what is important is that one is capable of love. It is perhaps the only glimpse we are permitted of eternity.
- Helen Hayes
(1900 -)
American actor, writer

A man when he is making up
to anybody can be cordial and
gallant and full of little
attentions and altogether
charming. But when a man is
really in love he can't help
looking like a sheep.
- Agatha Christie
(Dame Agatha Mary Clarissa
Miller Christie Mallowan,
1891 - 1976)
English detective story writer

Trouble is a part of your life, and if you don't share it, you don't give the person who loves you enough chance to love you enough.

> \- Dinah Shore
> (1920 - 1994)
> American singer, actress

Intimate relationships cannot substitute for a life plan. But to have any viability at all, a life plan must include intimate relationships.

> \- Harriet Lerner
> (20th c.)
> American therapist, writer

If love is the answer, could you please rephrase the question?

- Lily Tomlin
(1939)
American comedienne, actress

The only time a woman really succeeds in changing a man is when he's a baby.

- Natalie Wood
(1938 - 1982)
American actor

Sometimes idiosyncracies which used to be irritating become endearing, part of the complexity of a partner who has become woven deep into our own selves.
- Madeleine L'Engle
(1918 -)
American writer

I always felt that the great high privilege, relief, and comfort of friendship was that one had to explain nothing.
- Katherine Mansfield
(1888 - 1923)
New Zealand-born English writer

You can keep your friends by
not giving them away.
- Mary Pettibone Poole
(20th c.)
American writer

Writers seldom choose as
friends those self-contained
characters who are never in
trouble, never unhappy or ill,
never make mistakes, and
always count their change
when it's handed to them.
- Catherine Drinker Bowen
(1897 - 1973)
American historian,
biographer, essayist

Love at a distance may be more poignant; it is also idealized. Contact, more than separation, is the test of attachment.

- Ilka Chase
(1905 - 1978)
American writer, actress, radio/TV personality

No one can go it alone. Somewhere along the way is the person who gives you that job, who has faith that you can make it. And everyone has something to work for, if only he will look for it.

- Grace Gil Olivarez
(1928 -)
Mexican American social activist, attorney

If we would build on a sure foundation in friendship, we must love friends for their sake rather than for our own.
- Charlotte Bronte
(1816 - 1855)
English writer, poet

Nobody has ever measured, not even poets, how much the heart can hold.
- Zelda Fitzgerald
(1900 - 1948)
American writer, literary figure

One of the oldest human needs is having someone to wonder where you are when you don't come home at night.

> - Margaret Mead
> (1901 - 1977)
> American anthropologist, writer, editor, museum curator

We can only learn to love by loving.

> - Iris Murdoch
> (1919 -)
> Irish-born English novelist, philosopher

Love is something like the clouds that were in the sky before the sun came out. You cannot touch the clouds, you know; but you feel the rain and know how glad the flowers and the thirsty earth are to have it after a hot day. You cannot touch love either, but you feel the sweetness that it pours into everything.

- Anne Sullivan
(1866 - 1936)
American educator, teacher of Helen Keller

Love from one being to another can only be that two solitudes come nearer, recognize and protect and comfort each other.
- Han Suyin
(1917)
Chinese physician and writer

Love has pride in nothing - but its own humility.
- Clare Boothe Luce
(1903 -)
American diplomat and congresswoman

Other Hardcovers by Great Quotations

Other Titles by Great Quotations

GREAT QUOTATIONS PUBLISHING
1967 Quincy Court
Glendale Heights, IL 60139-2045
Phone (708) 582-2800, Fax (708) 582-2813